The Birth of Dawn Treader Christian School

Written by
NINA KAY GREGORY

Illustrations by
JAN DE SEE

The Marvelous Mill on Market Street
Written by Nina Kay Gregory
Illustrations by Jan De See
Cover Design by Caroline Cahoon
Edited by Catherine DeVries

Library of Congress
Text © 2025 by Nina Kay Gregory
Illustrations © 2025 by Jan De See
All rights reserved. No part of this book may be reproduced in any form without written permission from the publisher, except in the case of brief quotations embodied in critical articles and reviews.

ISBN 979-8-9992280-0-0

Dawn Treader Christian School & Great Falls Publishing
1 Market Street
Paterson, New Jersey 07501
www.dawntreaderchristian.org

Printed in the United States of America

To the Dawn Treader parents, faculty and board members who
welcomed and encouraged me as I first came to Dawn Treader, including
Al and Annetta Vander Lugt; Bud and Judi Terpstra; Karl and Jeannie Kammeraad;
Doug and Margaret Harrison; Karen and Charles Walker; Pastor John and Debra Algera;
Herb ("the man with the white hair" and ECUMP license plate) and Jane Van Denend; first principal
Fred Style ("the man with the beard" and orange Volkswagen); Wilma Knoll ("the small woman");
Pastor Stan ("the tall man") and Barb Vander Klay—and to so many other administrators,
colleagues, parents and students who joined the journey in subsequent years.

And to current Dawn Treader Board member Rob Skead,
without whose expertise and encouragement
this book would never have seen publication.

And to my husband, Dwight Gregory, who gave inspiration and ideas and
even some of the sentences to bring the book to completion originally, and
didn't give up until seeing it through to publication more than forty years later.

And to our sons, James and David (Dawn Treader alumni),
and our grandson, Marshal Gregory, an avid reader.

NKG

To Beverly—teacher, artist, friend.

JDS

THE YEAR 1977

The lonely old mill watched sadly day after day as the cars, trucks, and buses passed his corner. Sometimes they stopped at the diner across the street. Sometimes they stopped at the old factory across the other street. He heard children laughing as they walked to school. But nobody ever noticed him.

"Oh, if only someone would notice me," whined the mill. "Nobody seems to want an empty silk mill like me anymore. I'm so useless. I'm so ugly." Tears began to fall.

Forty years ago, his owners had turned off the machines. He had been almost empty ever since.

Two years ago, a man had tacked the "For Sale" sign onto his door. The old mill felt a glimmer of hope. Maybe now people would notice him.

Lately he had heard rumors about a new highway. It was supposed to be built right where he was sitting. He shuddered to think about what that meant for him.

Each day seemed so long. To help the time pass more quickly, he counted the cars. "87 Fords, 63 Buicks, 56 Toyotas, and one orange Volkswagen driven by a man with a beard." Everyone had somewhere to go. Some almost missed the stop sign.

Then one day it happened! The orange Volkswagen stayed longer than usual at the stop sign. The eyes of the man inside read the sign on the door. "For Sale. Archie Schwartz, Realtor." The man's face broke into a smile. The old mill couldn't understand. For two years he had been watching the same orange car stop at the same stop sign. What was different about today? What made the man with the beard smile? The mill saw a reflection in the window across the street. Nothing had changed. His windows were still covered with green plywood. His bricks were black and sooty from years of dirt and smoke.

After that day life seemed more exciting. Twice a day the little orange car would pass the mill. Twice a day the man with the beard would take a long look at the mill.

It was a warm spring night. The old mill watched the sun disappear over the Great Falls. He was feeling a bit sleepy himself when he heard faint voices. He felt a hand pat his side. Another hand jiggled the knob on his door.

"This is certainly the right spot," said a man with white hair. "There's plenty of room for everything," said the man with the keys.

Then they walked around the building and looked up and down at the mill's walls. The mill could no longer hear what they were saying.

Who were these people? the mill wondered. Suddenly he remembered the new highway. His heart stopped beating. They must be talking about tearing him down. He felt a cold chill. The mill watched the two men get into their cars and drive away. As the white Mercedes turned the corner, the mill could faintly make out the license plate—ECUMP. *E-C-U-M-P? ECUMP must be a demolition company!*

The mill couldn't sleep all night.

As the days passed, the old mill felt sadder than ever. Saturdays were saddest of all. This hot Saturday morning no children would be walking to school. On Saturdays the little orange car didn't go past. The mill's empty walls were hot and sweaty.

Then he felt something! Someone was pulling at the chains on his door. Several people were talking with excited voices. He wished they would slow down so he could understand what they were saying. Finally, a man took off the padlock and pushed open the squeaky door. When the sunlight showed their faces, the mill recognized the man with the white hair. Then he remembered the ECUMP license plate.

Oh no, thought the mill. *This must be the day. They've come to tear me down.*

"Watch out," exclaimed a woman as a loose board clattered to the floor. "Hand me a flashlight so I can see."

"Here. Use mine," volunteered another. Beams of light danced over the floors and up the walls.

"What a mess! I wonder how long it's been empty," said a lady.

"There must be six inches of dust on the floors. Watch out for the nails. And the mice."

"Here's a loose board covering the window," said a deep voice. "Help me pull it off so we'll have some light." They pulled and tugged until finally the board gave way.

"Oh, no. This is even worse than I imagined," said a small lady. "All the windows are broken out."

"Look over here," came a voice from the corner of the room. "There's a huge hole in the floor!"

"You're right," agreed a tall man. "That's where the water wheel was. These old silk mills used the power of water to run the machines."

The mill searched the parking lot for bulldozers and cranes. All he could see were small cars.

If this ECUMP company is going to tear me down, why don't they get it over with? thought the mill.

"Look at all this open space," shouted the man with the white hair. He seemed more excited than anyone. "I tell you, this is the place. This is absolutely the place!"

"Speaking from experience," a deep voice announced firmly, "it will take two years to have this building ready."

"But September is only two months away," moaned the small lady.

September? Two months? Ready for what? Will people be making silk ribbons here again? The mill's thoughts were interrupted again by the deep voice.

"Yes, this project will take at least two years. The sandblasting alone will take two months."

Everyone stopped talking. They walked across the floor. Then they were gone. The old mill didn't know what sandblasting was, but it sounded like it would hurt.

The next week the old mill was lonelier than ever. Nothing had changed. There went the cars. The trucks. The buses.

The July heat was worse than ever. Then he heard the gravel crunching. To his surprise he saw the car with the ECUMP license plate. Then he saw the little orange car and the man with the beard. *Could it be? Does he work for the demolition company too? I had hoped he would be my friend.* The old mill watched as the two men carried big machines inside. He watched them put on space suits.

What is going to happen? It wasn't long before he knew. "Ouch!" cried the mill as sand and water pierced his walls and ceilings. *Why are they doing this to me? Is this what they meant by sandblasting?*

More men in space suits came. Some even stayed all night and slept on his floors.

Oh, such pain, bemoaned the mill. *I can't take this for two years,* he thought as he remembered the words of the man with the deep voice. Men started taking down his outside stairway, piece by piece. Oh, how he wished they would bring a wrecking ball and finish him off quickly!

Every day new cars pulled into the mill's parking lot. He winced as people hammered nails into his walls. Men pulled the green plywood from his rotted window frames. Then they placed something clear and shiny into big openings. One man seemed to have the special job of sticking pipes into his floors and walls. The mill heard someone call this "plumbing."

Sandblasting. New windows. Plumbing. People are everywhere just like the old days, said the mill to himself. So many things were happening at the same time. The old mill still didn't understand, but he was beginning to like the change. People in the passing cars began to notice him. Some would smile and nod their heads in approval. Just as he was beaming with pride, he overheard two women talking.

"These old factory floors are too rough. They will never do for Dawn Treader."

"I have an idea. Let's go..."

The old mill couldn't hear any more. *Dawn Treader? Who's Dawn Treader?* wondered the old mill. *And what's wrong with my floors?*

Before long the same women appeared carrying stacks of soft, fluffy squares. Orange, blue, brown, green. Some with two, three, four colors in one square. The old mill heard the words "carpet samples." He liked them until the people began pounding carpet nails into his floors. *Ouch!*

The old mill was having trouble getting enough rest. People worked from early morning until late at night. They seemed as happy as if they were watching a dream come true. The old mill could hardly believe it himself. It was like a miracle! Still, he wondered why so many people would spend so many hours making him beautiful. Never in all his life had he heard so much laughter.

Crowded into a corner of his second floor were old tool bins, work tables, wash basins, and hundreds of silk bobbins.

Why are they saving these old things when everything else is so new and pretty? he wondered.

Late one afternoon, two young people began dragging a tool bin across his floor. *Ow, that hurts,* whined the mill. One of the young workers started washing the dirt off an old wash basin.

He said, "I think this wash basin should be painted red and the tool bin could be blue. You know how children love bright colors."

Children? What about children? wondered the mill.

The lady continued, "We need to find a stopper for this wash basin to keep the sand inside. That tool bin will make a great toy bin."

Then a truck arrived, and people brought in small desks and chairs.

Sand tables, tool bins, small chairs, and tables? Children? Then he knew. He was going to be a school! He felt a surge of pride. Children would soon walk through his doors to read and write, to sing and create.

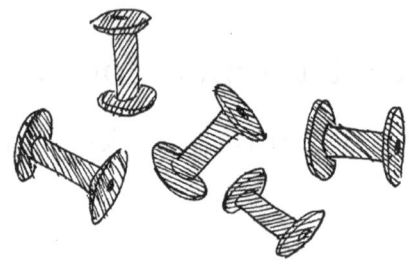

The summer was coming to an end. The old mill noticed that the man with the beard was unpacking boxes of books. He was writing on papers. New people came. They weren't wearing work clothes. The mill heard words like "curriculum, tuition, contracts, transportation."

"To God Be the Glory"

Late one Saturday night, men were working with torches and pieces of metal, making a new stairway up the back. The old mill heard the man with the white hair cry out, "Ouch, that was still hot." But he didn't hear anything else. He was exhausted and couldn't stay awake any longer.

The old mill woke up early the next morning and looked out his back window toward the big waterfall. He saw the orange Volkswagen, the car with the ECUMP license plate, and many more cars in the parking lot next to the statue of Alexander Hamilton.

The little parking lot was filling up with people. This had never happened at six o'clock on a Sunday morning. He heard guitars and singing, "Morning has broken."

Another man with a beard stood up to speak. The sound of water rushing over the falls muffled some of the words, but he heard the name "Dawn Treader" again. "People of the Son. Christian Urban Education. Traveling toward the Sunrise. Alternative school." More singing, "To God be the glory."

Then suddenly everyone from the park started walking across the street, up the new metal stairs, and into the old mill. In the fresh sunlight the mill noticed the words on a sign someone had hung the night before:

This must be the mill's new name! He looked at the words at the bottom of the sign. *So that's what ECUMP means!* the old mill said to himself.

There was laughing. Crying. Hugging. Lots of hugging. People were eating donuts and drinking coffee. Children were running around everywhere. Black children. White children. Brown children. Everyone was talking at once.

"This is marvelous."

"I counted fifteen colors on the floor."

"I counted twenty."

"It's a miracle."

"Look at this sandbox. What a clever idea!"

"Can you believe we got it ready in two months?"

"Have you ever seen such a big wooden table?"

The old mill heard someone talking about the big wooden spools hanging as decorations from the ceiling. "They were the bobbins once used to wind the silk thread made here."

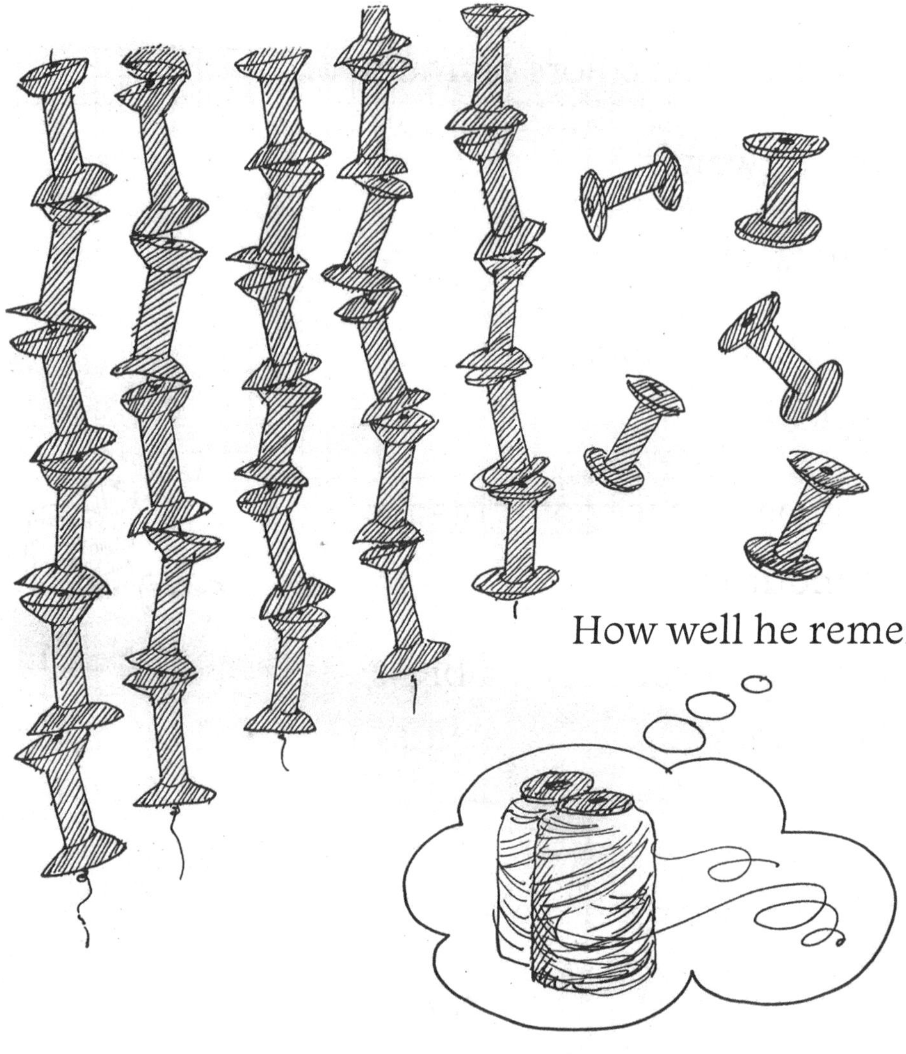

How well he remembered!

Since that celebration, now the mill was getting used to his new name and his new job. Five mornings a week, children pour out of vans and buses and scramble up the new stairs. They read. They write. They sing. They pray. They play with a guinea pig named Nibbles, a snake named Speedy, and a rabbit named Raspberry. They watch the tropical fish.

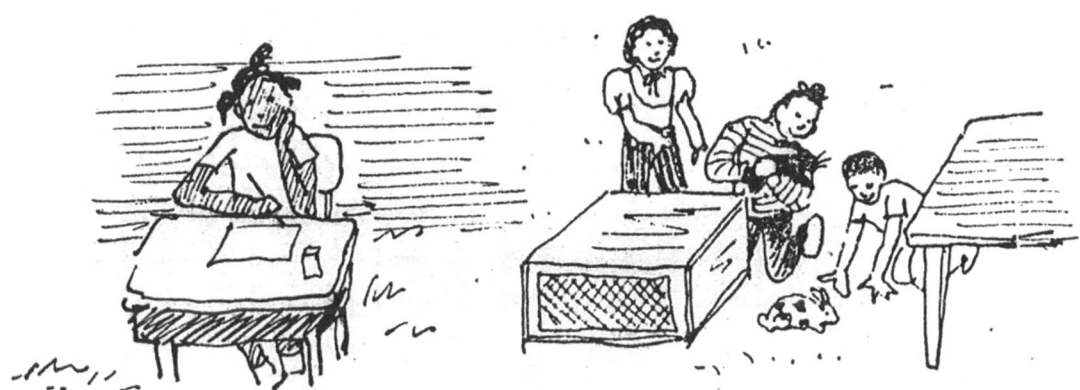

Small wooden blocks become bridges, skyscrapers, and cathedrals. Paintings, drawings, colorful quilts, and more of the children's creations decorate his walls.

Sometimes his whole frame aches from the pounding of children's feet and basketballs on his new fourth-floor gym. But their laughter makes him feel better. He feels useful.

The hammering still goes on. Every year the ECUMP people rearrange his inside walls or fix new rooms.

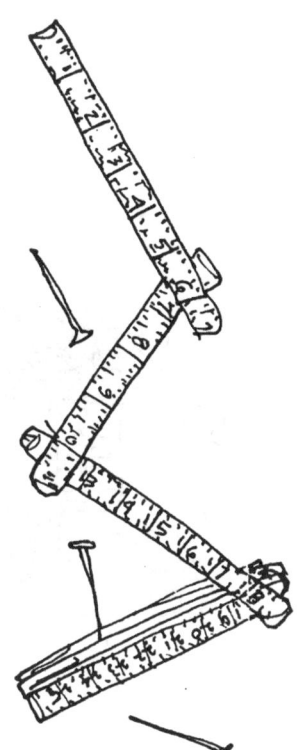

Every week a few strangers walk through. They look at the walls, the colorful floors, the bright sunlight streaming through the tall windows. They all say, "This is marvelous! I can't believe there's a school like this right in the middle of the old city."

Every Saturday, some of the children's parents come to clean the mill from top to bottom. And one of the teachers comes to feed Speedy and Nibbles and Rasberry. And the tropical fish!

Some other days, when the children have all gone home, a few of the big people sit in a circle in a classroom. They talk about problems. They talk about the "miracles." They talk to a "Father" that the mill still hasn't been able to see during those talks.

Every night, the sun slips down behind the waterfall to go to sleep. The warm glow starts to fade from his west wall. And each night he remembers a little bit less of his lonely days, because now he is beautiful and useful once again.

NOT THE END!

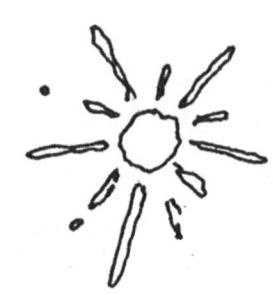

The Voyage Continues

Through the years, the old mill watched Dawn Treader, like the ship it was named after, experience its share of high seas and storms. He continued to hear many prayers to the "Father" within his walls and was so happy to see Dawn Treader weather through. The mill realized it was all because of God's grace and blessing that kept the school afloat and the students thriving. After all, the mill understood that Dawn Treader Christian School is God's school and that its students, faculty, administration, and supporters are God's children. God loves the city of Paterson! And he also loves the old mill!

The old mill smiled as he watched the school's journey. He made a special note in its "Ship's Log" in 2009 when Charles Salinas, a local pastor and former corrections officer, came on board as the school's executive director. At that time, the school was down to 26 students (that saddened the old mill because he remembered when the school opened its doors in 1977 with 70 students).

Since 2009, year after year, Dawn Treader grew again thanks to Pastor Charles' leadership and the Good Lord's kindness and blessing. *It's 2025 and we now have an enrollment of 109 students!* the old mill said to himself, gratefully. *And this crew of Dawn Treader has big goals for the future, all for God's glory.*

To empower our students to live relevantly for Christ and make a difference in the world.

Would you like to make this old mill happy and prosperous? Discover more about the school and how you can help enhance Dawn Treader students' educational experience and nurture their spiritual growth in a place where faith and learning go hand in hand. Just scan the QR Code to the right.

As a valued partner in the mission of Dawn Treader, your prayers and contributions help touch the lives of each student and expand their opportunities—and keep me (the old mill) beautiful and useful.

We are truly grateful for you and your generosity.

Thank you and I hope you enjoyed my story. To God be the glory!

the marvelous mill on market street

About This Book

Nina Kay Gregory taught in a variety of capacities at Dawn Treader Christian School from 1981 to 1991. She crafted this story in 1984 for a writing class at William Paterson University of New Jersey and partnered with Dawn Treader's newsletter designer Jan De See who created the art to accompany the story. They made a simple, homemade story that was shared with only a few people. Then, like the old mill, the story sat in a drawer lonely, sad, and useless for about 40 years. Until December 2024, when it was dusted off, polished, and transformed into this book for many more readers to enjoy! We hope the tale of the mill and school's history, mission, and influence—which continues today—has blessed you.

The Voyage of the Dawn Treader, by C.S. Lewis, tells the story of a ship which takes some children through many imaginative adventures in another world. Always traveling toward the sun, they finally arrive at a point where the realities of this world can be met in a Christian way.

Dawn Treader Christian School is in the historic district of Paterson, New Jersey, America's oldest planned industrial city. One block from the Great Falls of the Passaic River, where General George Washington, Alexander Hamilton, and Marquis de Lafayette once picnicked during the American Revolution, the school occupies the former Union Works/Rosen Mill building. It was built in 1827 and reconstructed in 1890. The school, founded in 1977 by the Evangelical Committee for Urban Ministries (ECUMP) in Paterson, has as its goal "to educate the total student in an intercultural Christian setting, so that as a unique image-bearer of God, each may live the Christian life."

Foundational Dawn Treader Bible Verses

"All your children shall be taught by the Lord,
and great shall be the peace of your children.

In righteousness you shall be established;
You shall be far from oppression, for you shall not fear;
And from terror, for it shall not come near you."

ISAIAH 54:13-14
New King James Version

"Train up a child in the way he should go,
and when he is old he will not depart from it."

PROVERBS 22:6
New King James Version

"Dawn Treaders are people of the Son.
In this living history lesson, brightness would
be woven into children's lives, so that with
Christ at the center of everything,
their voyage with Dawn Treader would,
we pray, empower them to live relevantly
for Christ in the real world."

STAN VANDER KLAY
One of the Founders of Dawn Treader Christian School